Advanced Image Analysis and Recognition

Stochastic Processes and Pattern Recognition in Image Processing

Laxmi Narayan Soni

Made with ❤on the Notion Press Platform

www.notionpress.com

Dedication

This book is dedicated to my family, mentors, colleagues, and students, whose unwavering support, guidance, and encouragement have been invaluable throughout my journey. Their insights and inspiration have shaped this work, and I am deeply grateful for their presence in my life.

To all researchers and learners exploring the world of stochastic processes and pattern recognition in image processing, may this book serve as a stepping stone toward innovation and discovery.

Laxmi Narayan Soni

Contents

Foreword

In the ever-evolving field of image processing, the integration of stochastic processes and pattern recognition has significantly transformed how we analyze and interpret visual data. This book, Stochastic Processes and Pattern Recognition in Image Processing, by Laxmi Narayan Soni, delves into these critical areas, bridging foundational theories with modern computational techniques.

The increasing reliance on artificial intelligence, machine learning, and probabilistic modeling in image analysis underscores the relevance of this work. The book covers both the mathematical underpinnings and practical applications, making it an essential resource for students, researchers, and professionals seeking to deepen their understanding of robust image analysis techniques.

Laxmi Narayan Soni's expertise in digital electronics, image processing, and AI-driven research is reflected in the depth and clarity of this book. His ability to integrate theoretical rigor with real-world applications makes this work particularly valuable. Whether one is a novice stepping into the field or an expert exploring advanced methodologies, this book serves as a comprehensive guide to stochastic modeling and pattern recognition techniques in image processing.

I congratulate the author on this excellent contribution and encourage readers to explore the innovative approaches presented in this book.

Laxmi Narayan Soni

Assistant Professor

2025

Preface

The field of image processing is rapidly evolving, driven by advancements in artificial intelligence, stochastic modeling, and pattern recognition. This book, Stochastic Processes and Pattern Recognition in Image Processing, is the culmination of years of research, teaching, and collaboration. It aims to bridge the gap between theoretical foundations and practical applications, making it a valuable resource for students, researchers, and professionals in the domain of computer.

Throughout this book, I have explored how stochastic processes provide a robust framework for analyzing the randomness inherent in image data. From Markov processes and Bayesian methods to probabilistic graphical models and deep learning, the book delves into techniques essential for pattern recognition and advanced image processing. Each chapter is structured to offer a comprehensive understanding of both the mathematical concepts.

The motivation behind writing this book stems from my experience as an educator and researcher, where I witnessed the increasing demand for stochastic approaches in modern image-processing applications. The journey of compiling this work has been enriched by discussions with colleagues, contributions from students, and insights gained from industry collaborations. I am immensely grateful to those who have supported and inspired me throughout this endeavor.

I hope this book serves as a guiding resource for readers eager to explore the depths of stochastic modeling and pattern recognition in image processing. Whether you are delving into this field for academic research or developing cutting-edge applications, may this work ignite curiosity and drive innovation.

Laxmi Narayan Soni

Acknowledgments

This book is the result of years of dedication, research, and collaboration, and I am deeply grateful to those who have supported and guided me throughout this journey.

First and foremost, I extend my sincere gratitude to my mentors and colleagues, whose invaluable insights and encouragement have greatly influenced the depth and quality of this work. Their expertise and feedback have helped shape the content, ensuring a comprehensive and practical approach to stochastic processes and pattern recognition in image processing.

I would also like to express my appreciation to my students, whose curiosity and enthusiasm for learning have been a constant source of inspiration. Their engagement and thought-provoking questions have contributed to refining the clarity and applicability of the concepts discussed in this book.

A heartfelt thank you to my family and friends, whose unwavering support and patience have been instrumental in making this book possible. Their encouragement and belief in my work have kept me motivated through every challenge.

Finally, I acknowledge the contributions of the scientific community and researchers, whose pioneering work in image processing, AI, and stochastic modeling has laid the foundation for this book. Their research and innovations continue to inspire new possibilities in the field.

To everyone who has been a part of this journey, I extend my deepest gratitude. This book is a testament to the collective knowledge and efforts of many, and I hope it serves as a valuable resource for all who explore its pages.

Introduction

In the modern era of artificial intelligence and digital transformation, image processing has emerged as a critical domain with applications spanning medical imaging, autonomous systems, surveillance, remote sensing, and industrial automation. As the complexity of image data increases, the need for robust mathematical models to analyze and interpret visual information has become more significant than ever. This book, Stochastic Processes and Pattern Recognition in Image Processing, provides a comprehensive exploration of how stochastic methods and pattern recognition techniques enhance image analysis, recognition, and classification.

Stochastic processes offer a probabilistic framework for handling the uncertainty and randomness inherent in real-world images. From Markov random fields and Bayesian models to probabilistic deep learning techniques, this book delves into the fundamental principles and practical applications of stochastic modeling in image processing. Pattern recognition, on the other hand, forms the backbone of computer vision, enabling machines to detect, classify, and interpret patterns with precision.

This book is structured to provide both theoretical foundations and hands-on applications, making it a valuable resource for students, researchers, and professionals in fields like computer science, electrical engineering, and artificial intelligence. Each chapter systematically introduces key concepts, mathematical formulations, and real-world case studies, ensuring a holistic learning experience for readers at various levels of expertise.

The motivation behind this book is to bridge the gap between classical stochastic models and modern AI-driven image processing techniques. Whether you are exploring fundamental concepts of probability in image analysis or implementing deep learning models for complex pattern recognition tasks, this book offers the necessary tools and insights to advance your knowledge in the field.

As technology continues to evolve, the synergy between stochastic processes and pattern recognition will play an even more significant role in shaping the future of intelligent image analysis. This book aims to equip readers with the skills and methodologies needed to tackle challenges and innovate in this exciting domain.

1. Introduction to Stochastic Processes in Image Processing

1.1 Overview

Stochastic processes play a fundamental role in image processing, where the data's uncertainty and variability are inherent. These processes provide powerful tools for modelling, analyzing, and interpreting the random nature of image data. This chapter introduces the fundamental concepts of stochastic processes, their mathematical foundations, and their applications in image processing.

1.2 Stochastic Processes: Definitions and Key Concepts

A stochastic process is a collection of random variables $\{X(t): t \in T\}$ indexed by a set T, typically representing time or space. In image processing, T can represent the spatial coordinates of an image. Fundamental properties and types of stochastic processes include:

1.2.1 Random Variables and Distributions

A random variable X is a function that assigns an actual number to each outcome in a sample space. The Distribution of X describes the probabilities of its possible values. Standard distributions in image processing include:

- Gaussian Distribution: $X \sim N(\mu, \sigma^2)$, where μ is the mean and σ^2 is the variance.
- Poisson Distribution: $P(X = k) = \frac{\lambda^k e^{-\lambda}}{k!}$, used for modeling count-based phenomena.

1.2.2 Markov Processes

A Markov process is a stochastic process with the Markov property: the future state depends only on the present state, not on the past states. Formally, $P(X_{t+1} \mid X_t, X_{t-1}, \dots\dots, X0) = P(X_{t+1} \mid X_t)$

1.2.3 Stationary Processes

A stationary process has statistical properties that do not change over time. For a process $\{X(t)\}$, it is stationary if $E[X(t)] = \mu$ and $Cov(X(t), X(t + \tau)) = \gamma(\tau)$, independent of t.

1.3 Mathematical Formulation of Stochastic Processes

1.3.1 Probability Density Functions and Expected Value

The probability density function (PDF) $fX(x)$ describes the likelihood of a continuous random variable X taking a specific value x. The expected value (mean) $E[X]$ is given by:

$$E[X] = \int_{-\infty}^{\infty} x f_X(x)\, dx$$

1.3.2 Covariance and Correlation Functions

The covariance function $Cov(X(t), X(s))$ measures the joint variability of two random variables at times t and s:

$$Cov(X(t), X(s)) = E[(X(t) - \mu_t)(X(s) - \mu_s)]$$

The correlation function $\rho X(t), X(s)$ is the normalized form:

$$\rho X(t), X(s) = \frac{Cov\big(X(t), X(s)\big)}{\mu_t \mu_s}$$

1.3.3 Power Spectral Density

The power spectral density (PSD) describes how the power of a signal is distributed with frequency. For a stationary process $X(t)$, the PSD $S_x(f)$ is the Fourier transform of the autocorrelation function $R_X(\tau)$:

$$S_x(f) = \int_{-\infty}^{\infty} R_X(\tau) e^{-j2\pi f\tau \, d\tau} d\tau$$

1.4 Stochastic Models in Image Processing

1.4.1 Gaussian Random Fields

A Gaussian Random Field (GRF) is a generalization of the Gaussian process to multiple dimensions, often used to model spatial data such as images. For a random field $\{X(s) : s \in R^2\}$, any finite subset follows a multivariate Gaussian distribution.

1.4.1.1 Mean and Covariance Function

For a GRF $X(s)$ with mean function $m(s)$ and covariance function $C(s, s')$:

$$m(s) = E[X(s)]$$

$$C(s, s') = E[(X(s) - m(s))(X(s') - m(s'))]$$

1.4.2 Markov Random Fields

A Markov Random Field (MRF) is a set of random variables having a Markov property described by an undirected graph. In image processing, MRFs are used for modeling spatial dependencies.

1.4.2.1 Hammersley-Clifford Theorem

The Hammersley-Clifford theorem states that a random field X is a MRF if and only if its probability distribution can be factorized according to the cliques of the graph G:

$$P(X) = \frac{1}{Z} \prod_{C \in C} \psi C(X_c)$$

where Z is the partition function, C is the set of cliques, and ψC are the potential functions.

1.5 Applications in Image Processing

1.5.1 Image Denoising

Image denoising aims to remove noise while preserving important features. A common approach is to model the noisy image Y as:

$$Y = X + N$$

where X is the original image and N is the noise, often modeled as Gaussian. Denoising can be achieved by estimating X using techniques like Wiener filtering:

$$\dot{\hat{X}}(f) = \frac{S_X(f)}{S_X(f) + S_N(f)} Y(f)$$

1.5.2 Image Segmentation

Image segmentation partitions an image into regions with similar properties. MRFs are particularly effective, where the segmentation S is modeled to maximize the posterior probability $P(S \mid I)$:

$$P(S \mid I) \propto P(I \mid S)\, P(S)\, P(S \mid I)$$

Here, $P(I \mid S)$ is the likelihood, and $P(S)$ is the prior modeled by an MRF.

1.5.3 Texture Analysis

Textures are patterns in images that can be modeled using stochastic processes. A common model is the autoregressive (AR) model, where each pixel is a linear combination of its neighbors plus noise:

$$X(s) = \sum_{r \in N_s} a_r X(s-r) + \epsilon(s)$$

where N_s is the neighborhood of s, ara_rar are the coefficients, and $\epsilon(s)$ is white noise.

1.6 Conclusion

Stochastic processes provide a robust framework for modeling and analyzing the randomness inherent in image data. From Gaussian random fields to Markov random fields, these processes enable effective solutions for various image processing tasks, including denoising, segmentation, and texture analysis. Understanding the mathematical underpinnings of these models is crucial for developing advanced image processing algorithms.

References

1. A. Papoulis, S. U. Pillai, "Probability, Random Variables, and Stochastic Processes," McGraw-Hill, 2002.
2. R. Chellappa, A. K. Jain, "Markov Random Fields: Theory and Applications," Academic Press, 1993.
3. J. S. Lim, "Two-Dimensional Signal and Image Processing," Prentice Hall, 1990.

2. Fundamentals of Pattern Recognition

2.1 Overview

Pattern recognition is a critical field within image processing and computer vision, focused on classifying data based on patterns and statistical information. This chapter delves into the fundamental concepts, mathematical formulations, and practical implementations of pattern recognition, including feature extraction, classification techniques, and evaluation metrics. Examples and MATLAB programs are provided to illustrate key concepts.

2.2 Key Concepts in Pattern Recognition

2.2.1 Patterns and Features

A pattern is a set of data that represents an entity. Features are measurable attributes or characteristics extracted from a pattern. The process involves converting raw data into a form that can be analyzed to identify patterns.

2.2.1.1 Feature Vector

A feature vector x\mathbf{x}x is a n-dimensional vector of numerical features that represent an object:

$$X = [\, x_1, x_2, \dots, x_n]$$

where x_i are the individual features.

2.2.2 Classification

Classification assigns a pattern to one of several predefined classes. This can be formulated as a mapping from the feature space R^n to a finite set of labels $\{1,2,\dots,C\}$.

2.2.2.1 Decision Boundaries

Decision boundaries separate the feature space into regions corresponding to different classes. Mathematically, a decision boundary can be represented by a function $f(x) = 0$.

2.2.3 Learning Paradigms

2.2.3.1 Supervised Learning

In supervised learning, a classifier is trained using labeled data. The objective is to learn a function $h : R^n \rightarrow \{1, 2, \dots, C\}$ that maps feature vectors to class labels.

2.2.3.2 Unsupervised Learning

Unsupervised learning involves finding patterns in unlabeled data. Clustering algorithms, such as K-means, are common techniques used to group similar patterns.

2.3 Feature Extraction

2.3.1 Dimensionality Reduction

Dimensionality reduction techniques transform high-dimensional data into a lower-dimensional space, preserving essential features while reducing computational complexity.

2.3.1.1 Principal Component Analysis (PCA)

Principal Component Analysis (PCA) identifies the directions (principal components) in which the variance of the data is maximized. The transformation matrix W is composed of the eigenvectors of the covariance matrix Σ:

$$W = [w_1, w_2, \dots, w_k]$$

where w_i are the eigenvectors corresponding to the largest eigenvalues.

2.3.2 Feature Selection

Feature selection involves selecting a subset of relevant features for building robust learning models. Methods include filter, wrapper, and embedded techniques.

2.3.2.1 Fisher's Linear Discriminant

Fisher's Linear Discriminant aims to find a linear combination of features that separates two or more classes. For two classes, the Fisher criterion $J(w)$ is:

$$J(W) = \frac{w^T S_B w}{w^T S_w w}$$

where S_B and S_w are the between-class and within-class scatter matrices, respectively.

2.4 Classification Techniques

2.4.1 Bayesian Classifiers

Bayesian classifiers apply Bayes' theorem to compute the posterior probability of each class given the observed data.

2.4.1.1 Naive Bayes Classifier

The Naive Bayes classifier assumes feature independence:

$$P(C_k|X) = \frac{P(x|C_k)P(C_k)}{P(x)}$$

Classification is performed by selecting the class with the highest posterior probability:

$$\hat{y} = \arg max_k \; P(C_k) \prod_{i=1}^{n} P\,(x_i \mid C_k)$$

2.4.2 Linear Discriminant Analysis (LDA)

Linear Discriminant Analysis (LDA) finds a linear combination of features that best separates multiple classes. The decision function is:

$$f(x) = w^T x + b$$

Where w is the weight vector and b is the bias.

2.4.3 Support Vector Machines (SVM)

Support Vector Machines (SVM) aim to find the hyperplane that maximizes the margin between two classes. The optimization problem is:

$$min_{w,b} \frac{1}{2} ||W||^2$$

Subject to $y_i \ (W^T X_i + b) \ \geq 1, i = 1, \dots \dots N$

MATLAB Implementation: SVM

```
% Generate synthetic data

rng('default');

numPoints = 100;

X = [randn(numPoints,2)*0.75+ones(numPoints,2);
randn(numPoints,2)*0.5-ones(numPoints,2)];

Y = [ones(numPoints,1); -ones(numPoints,1)];

% Train SVM classifier

SVMModel = fitcsvm(X,Y);

% Plot decision boundary

d = 0.02;

[x1Grid, x2Grid] = meshgrid(min(X(:,1)):d:max(X(:,1)),
min(X(:,2)):d:max(X(:,2)));

xGrid = [x1Grid(:), x2Grid(:)];

[~, scores] = predict(SVMModel, xGrid);

figure;
```

```
gscatter(X(:,1), X(:,2), Y, 'rb', 'oo');

hold on;

contour(x1Grid, x2Grid, reshape(scores(:,2), size(x1Grid)), [0 0], 'k');

legend({'Class 1', 'Class 2', 'Decision Boundary'});

title('Support Vector Machine Decision Boundary');

hold off;
```

2.5 Evaluation Metrics

2.5.1 Confusion Matrix

A confusion matrix is used to evaluate the performance of a classifier by comparing actual and predicted classifications.

	Predicted Positive	Predicted Negative
Actual Positive	TP	FN
Actual Negative	TP	TN

2.5.2 Accuracy, Precision, Recall, and F1 Score

- Accuracy: Accuracy = $\frac{TP + TN}{TP + TN + FP + FN}$
- Precision: Precision = $\frac{TP}{TP + FP}$
- Recall: Recall = $\frac{TP}{TP + FP}$
- F1 Score: F1 Score = $\frac{2\ .\ Precision\ .\ Recall}{Precision + Recall}$

2.5.3 Receiver Operating Characteristic (ROC) Curve

The ROC curve plots the true positive rate (TPR) against the false positive rate (FPR) at various threshold settings. The area under the ROC curve (AUC) is a measure of the classifier's performance.

MATLAB Implementation: ROC Curve

```
% Generate synthetic data for ROC curve

rng('default');

scores = [randn(100,1); randn(100,1)+1];

labels = [zeros(100,1); ones(100,1)];

% Calculate ROC curve

[X,Y,T,AUC] = perfcurve(labels, scores, 1);

figure;

plot(X,Y);

xlabel('False positive rate');

ylabel('True positive rate');

title('ROC Curve');

legend(['AUC = ' num2str(AUC)]);
```

2.6 Applications in Image Processing

2.6.1 Face Recognition

Face recognition involves identifying or verifying a person from an image. Techniques include eigenfaces (PCA) and Fisherfaces (LDA).

2.6.2 Object Detection

Object detection identifies and locates objects within an image. Techniques such as Haar cascades and deep learning models like YOLO (You Only Look Once) are widely used.

2.6.3 Handwriting Recognition

Handwriting recognition converts handwritten text into digital form. It utilizes feature extraction methods and classifiers such as SVMs and neural networks.

2.7 Conclusion

Pattern recognition is a cornerstone of image processing, providing tools and techniques necessary to classify and interpret visual data. Understanding these fundamentals is essential for developing robust and effective image processing systems.

References

1. R. O. Duda, P. E. Hart, D. G. Stork, "Pattern Classification," Wiley-Interscience, 2000.
2. C. M. Bishop, "Pattern Recognition and Machine Learning," Springer, 2006.
3. S. Theodoridis, K. Koutroumbas, "Pattern Recognition," Academic Press, 2008.

3. Random Fields and Image Modeling

3.1 Overview

Random fields play a critical role in modeling spatial dependencies in image data. They provide a robust mathematical framework for representing and analyzing the stochastic nature of images. This chapter delves into the fundamental concepts of random fields, their properties, and their application in image modeling, including Markov Random Fields (MRFs) and Gaussian Random Fields (GRFs).

3.2 Random Fields: Definitions and Properties

3.2.1 Definition of a Random Field

A random field is a collection of random variables indexed by a multi-dimensional space, typically representing spatial or temporal domains. Formally, a random field $X(s)$ is defined as:

$$\{X(s): s \in S\}$$

where S is a spatial domain, and $X(s)$ represents the random variable at location s.

3.2.2 Types of Random Fields

3.2.2.1 Discrete and Continuous Random Fields

- Discrete Random Fields: The spatial domain S consists of a finite set of points, often representing pixels in an image.
- Continuous Random Fields: The spatial domain S is continuous, which can be used for modeling continuous spatial phenomena.

3.2.3 Stationarity and Isotropy

- Stationarity: A random field is stationary if its statistical properties are invariant under translations in the spatial domain.
- Isotropy: A random field is isotropic if its statistical properties are invariant under rotations.

3.2.4 Covariance Function

The covariance function $C(s,t)$ of a random field $X(s)$ is defined as:

$$C(s,t) = Cov(X(s), X(t))$$

For a stationary random field, the covariance function depends only on the difference $h = s - t$.

$$C(s,t) = C(h)$$

Figure 3.1: Covariance Function Illustration

3.3 Markov Random Fields (MRFs)

3.3.1 Definition and Properties

A Markov Random Field (MRF) is a random field that satisfies the Markov property: the value of a variable at a given location depends only on its neighbors. Formally, X is an MRF if:

$$P\,(X_i \mid X_{-i}) = P\,(X_i \mid XN_{(i)})$$

Where $N_{(i)}$ denotes the set of neighbours of site iii.

3.3.2 Hammersley-Clifford Theorem

The Hammersley-Clifford theorem states that a Gibbs distribution can equivalently represent an MRF:

$$P(X = x) = \frac{1}{Z} exp(-\sum 1_{C \in C} V_c(X_c))$$

where C is the set of cliques, V_c is the potential function, and Z is the partition function.

3.3.3 Applications in Image Modeling

MRFs are widely used in image processing for tasks such as image segmentation, restoration, and texture modeling. They provide a powerful framework for incorporating spatial dependencies and context.

3.4 Gaussian Random Fields (GRFs)

3.4.1 Definition and Properties

A Gaussian Random Field (GRF) is a random field where any finite collection of random variables follows a multivariate Gaussian distribution. A GRF $X(s)$ is characterized by its mean function $\mu(s)$ and covariance function $C\ (s,t)$:

$$X(s) \sim N(\mu(s), C(s,t))$$

3.4.2 Covariance Models

Common covariance models for GRFs include:

- Exponential Covariance: $C(h) = \sigma^2 \exp(-\frac{|h|}{\lambda})$
- Gaussian Covariance: $C(h) = \sigma^2 \exp(-\frac{h^2}{2\lambda^2})$

3.4.3 Applications in Image Modeling

GRFs are used for modeling spatially continuous phenomena in images, such as terrain elevation and temperature distributions. They are also employed in kriging for geostatistical modeling and spatial interpolation.

3.5 Image Modeling with Random Fields

3.5.1 Texture Modeling

Random fields are essential for texture modeling in images. MRFs, in particular, are used to model the spatial dependencies in texture patterns.

The parameters of the random field can be estimated from the image data, allowing for realistic texture synthesis.

3.5.2 Image Segmentation

In image segmentation, random fields are used to model the spatial coherence of regions. MRFs provide a probabilistic framework for segmenting an image into meaningful regions by maximizing the posterior probability of the segmentation given the observed data.

3.5.3 Image Denoising

Random fields are employed in image denoising to model the smoothness of the image. By incorporating prior knowledge about the spatial structure of the image, random fields help in removing noise while preserving important features.

3.6 MATLAB Implementation: MRF for Image Segmentation

3.6.1 MATLAB Code

The following MATLAB code demonstrates the use of MRFs for image segmentation:

```
% Load an image
I = imread('image.jpg');
I = rgb2gray(I);
I = im2double(I);
% Define MRF parameters
beta = 1.0;  % Smoothness parameter
numIter = 20;  % Number of iterations
% Initialize labels randomly
lbel = randi([1, 2], size(I));
```

```
% Iterate to update labels
for iter = 1:numIter
    for i = 2:size(I,1)-1
        for j = 2:size(I,2)-1
            % Compute energy for each label
            E1 = -beta * (labels(i-1,j) + labels(i+1,j) + labels(i,j-1) +
labels(i,j+1) == 1);
            E2 = -beta * (labels(i-1,j) + labels(i+1,j) + labels(i,j-1) +
labels(i,j+1) == 2);
            % Update label
            if E1 < E2
                labels(i,j) = 1;
            else
                labels(i,j) = 2;
            end
        end
    end
end
% Display the segmented image
imshow(label2rgb(labels));
title('Segmented Image using MRF');
```

3.7 Conclusion

Random fields provide a versatile and powerful framework for image modeling, enabling the incorporation of spatial dependencies and probabilistic reasoning. By leveraging the properties of MRFs and GRFs, we can develop advanced techniques for image analysis, segmentation, and synthesis.

References

1. Besag, J. (1974). Spatial interaction and the statistical analysis of lattice systems. Journal of the Royal Statistical Society: Series B (Methodological), 36(2), 192-236.

2. Geman, S., & Geman, D. (1984). Stochastic relaxation, Gibbs distributions, and the Bayesian restoration of images. IEEE Transactions on Pattern Analysis and Machine Intelligence, (6), 721-741.

3. Rue, H., & Held, L. (2005). Gaussian Markov Random Fields: Theory and Applications. CRC Press.

4. Kindermann, R., & Snell, J. L. (1980). Markov Random Fields and Their Applications. American Mathematical Society.

5. Winkler, G. (2003). Image Analysis, Random Fields and Dynamic Monte Carlo Methods: A Mathematical Introduction. Springer Science & Business Media.

4. Pattern Recognition in Noisy Environments

4.1 Introduction

Pattern recognition in noisy environments is a challenging yet crucial aspect of image processing and computer vision. Noise, defined as any unwanted or random disturbance in an image, can significantly degrade the performance of pattern recognition systems. This chapter explores various techniques and methodologies to effectively recognize patterns amidst noise, ensuring reliable and accurate results.

4.2 Types of Noise

4.2.1 Gaussian Noise

Gaussian noise is one of the most common types, characterized by its normal Distribution. It can arise from various sources such as sensor imperfections and environmental conditions.

4.2.2 Salt-and-Pepper Noise

Salt-and-pepper noise manifests as random occurrences of black and white pixels, often caused by bit errors during transmission or switching mechanisms in digital circuits.

4.2.3 Speckle Noise

Speckle noise, particularly relevant in coherent imaging systems like radar and ultrasound, results from random variations in the return signal.

4.2.4 Poisson Noise

Poisson noise, also known as shot noise, is associated with variations in the number of photons detected, making it significant in low-light imaging scenarios.

4.3 Noise Reduction Techniques

4.3.1 Filtering

Filtering is a primary method for noise reduction. Common techniques include:

- Mean Filtering: Averages pixel values within a neighborhood to reduce noise.
- Median Filtering: Replaces each pixel with the median of its neighborhood, effectively reducing salt-and-pepper noise.
- Gaussian Filtering: Applies a Gaussian function to smooth the image while preserving edges.

4.3.2 Wavelet Transform

The wavelet transform decomposes an image into different frequency components, allowing for effective noise reduction by thresholding the wavelet coefficients.

4.3.3 Principal Component Analysis (PCA)

PCA reduces noise by transforming the image data into a set of orthogonal components, retaining the most significant features while discarding noise-dominated components.

4.4 Robust Pattern Recognition Techniques

4.4.1 Feature Extraction in Noisy Environments

Effective feature extraction is critical for robust pattern recognition. Techniques such as edge detection, corner detection, and texture analysis must be adapted to handle noise.

4.4.2 Statistical Pattern Recognition

Statistical methods, including Bayesian classification and hidden Markov models, leverage probabilistic frameworks to account for noise variability.

4.4.3 Machine Learning Approaches

Machine learning algorithms, particularly deep learning, have shown remarkable resilience to noise. Techniques such as convolutional neural networks (CNNs) and recurrent neural networks (RNNs) are trained on noisy data to improve robustness.

4.4.4 Ensemble Methods

Ensemble methods, such as bagging and boosting, combine multiple classifiers to enhance pattern recognition performance in noisy environments.

4.5 Case Studies and Applications

4.5.1 Medical Imaging

In medical imaging, noise can obscure critical details. Techniques like adaptive filtering and machine learning have improved the detection of anomalies in noisy medical scans.

4.5.2 Remote Sensing

Remote sensing applications must contend with noise from atmospheric interference and sensor limitations. Advanced noise reduction and pattern recognition techniques are essential for accurate environmental monitoring.

4.5.3 Industrial Inspection

In industrial inspection, noise can affect the detection of defects. Robust pattern recognition algorithms ensure reliable quality control in manufacturing processes.

4.6 Future Directions

Research continues to advance in developing more sophisticated techniques for pattern recognition in noisy environments. Emerging areas include quantum noise reduction methods, advanced neural architectures, and the integration of multimodal data sources.

4.7 Conclusion

Pattern recognition in noisy environments remains a vital and evolving field. By leveraging advanced noise reduction techniques and robust pattern recognition algorithms, we can achieve accurate and reliable results across various applications.

References

1. Gonzalez, R. C., & Woods, R. E. (2018). Digital Image Processing (4th ed.). Pearson.

2. Bishop, C. M. (2006). Pattern Recognition and Machine Learning. Springer.

3. Jain, A. K., Duin, R. P. W., & Mao, J. (2000). Statistical pattern recognition: A review. IEEE Transactions on Pattern Analysis and Machine Intelligence, 22(1), 4-37.

4. Lim, J. S. (1990). Two-Dimensional Signal and Image Processing. Prentice Hall.

5. Haralick, R. M., & Shapiro, L. G. (1992). Computer and Robot Vision (Vol. 1). Addison-Wesley.

5. Pattern Recognition in Noisy Environments

5.1 Introduction

Image segmentation is a fundamental task in image processing and computer vision, aimed at partitioning an image into meaningful regions. Among various segmentation techniques, random walks offer a probabilistic approach that effectively segments images by modeling pixel relationships as a stochastic process. This chapter explores the theory, application, advantages, and limitations of using random walks for image segmentation.

5.2 Fundamentals of Random Walks

5.2.1 Definition and Basic Concepts

A random walk is a mathematical process that describes a path consisting of successive random steps. In the context of image segmentation, this can be visualized as a pixel traversing the image grid, making probabilistic decisions about which neighboring pixel to move to next. This approach allows pixels with similar properties, such as intensity or texture, to be grouped into the same region.

5.2.2 Transition Probabilities

In image segmentation, transition probabilities define the likelihood of moving from one pixel to another based on their similarity. Typically, pixels with closer intensity values have a higher probability of being in the same segment, while those with significant differences are less likely to belong together. These probabilities are computed using pixel intensities, edges, and neighborhood structures.

5.2.3 Laplacian Matrix

The Laplacian matrix is a key component in the random walk algorithm. It represents the overall connectivity between pixels in an image by considering their similarities. This matrix helps in determining how information propagates across the image, ensuring that the segmentation process respects the inherent structure of the image.

5.3 Random Walks for Image Segmentation

5.3.1 The Random Walks Algorithm

The random walks algorithm for image segmentation follows a structured approach:

Graph Construction – The image is represented as a weighted graph, where each pixel is a node, and edges between nodes indicate the similarity between neighboring pixels.

Seed Selection – A set of seed points is chosen for each segment. These can be manually assigned or determined automatically using prior information.

Probability Calculation – The probability of a pixel belonging to a specific segment is computed by analyzing the connectivity and similarity between pixels.

Label Assignment – Each pixel is assigned to the segment corresponding to the seed with the highest probability, ensuring accurate segmentation.

5.3.2 Mathematical Formulation

The segmentation process relies on solving a system of equations that assigns each pixel to a segment based on predefined constraints. By using seed points and analyzing pixel similarities, the random walk algorithm determines the most likely segmentation for the image.

5.3.3 Algorithm Implementation

The random walks algorithm can be implemented efficiently using sparse matrix solvers for the Laplacian matrix. Here is a simplified MATLAB code snippet:

```
function labels = random_walker(image, seeds, labels)
    % Convert image to grayscale
    gray_image = rgb2gray(image);
    % Build weight matrix
    W = build_weight_matrix(gray_image);
    % Compute the Laplacian matrix
    D = diag(sum(W, 2));
    L = D – W
% Solve for probabilities
    u = zeros(size(gray_image));
    u(seeds) = labels(seeds);
    u(~seeds) = L(~seeds, ~seeds) \ (-L(~seeds, seeds) * u(seeds));
    % Assign labels based on probabilities
    [~, labels] = max(u, [], 2);
end
    function W = build_weight_matrix(image)
    % Define weight function based on pixel intensities
    sigma = 10;  % Control the influence of pixel intensity differences
    [rows, cols] = size(image);
    W = sparse(rows * cols, rows * cols);
```

```
    for i = 1:rows
        for j = 1:cols
            idx = sub2ind([rows, cols], i, j);
            neighbors = get_neighbors(i, j, rows, cols);
            for k = 1:numel(neighbors)
                n_idx = sub2ind([rows, cols], neighbors(k,1), neighbors(k,2));
                W(idx, n_idx) = exp(-abs(image(i,j) - image(neighbors(k,1),
neighbors(k,2)))^2 / (2 * sigma^2));
            end
        end
    end
end
% Solve for probabilities
    u = zeros(size(gray_image));
    u(seeds) = labels(seeds);
    u(~seeds) = L(~seeds, ~seeds) \ (-L(~seeds, seeds) * u(seeds));
    % Assign labels based on probabilities
    [~, labels] = max(u, [], 2);
end
    function W = build_weight_matrix(image)
    % Define weight function based on pixel intensities
    sigma = 10;  % Control the influence of pixel intensity differences
    [rows, cols] = size(image);
    W = sparse(rows * cols, rows * cols);
```

```
for i = 1:rows
    for j = 1:cols
        idx = sub2ind([rows, cols], i, j);
        neighbors = get_neighbors(i, j, rows, cols);
        for k = 1:numel(neighbors)
            n_idx = sub2ind([rows, cols], neighbors(k,1), neighbors(k,2));
            W(idx, n_idx) = exp(-abs(image(i,j) - image(neighbors(k,1), neighbors(k,2)))^2 / (2 * sigma^2));
        end
    end
end
end
```

5.4 Applications of Random Walks in Image Segmentation

5.4.1 Medical Imaging

Random walks have been widely used in medical imaging for segmenting anatomical structures such as organs and tumors. The probabilistic framework of random walks ensures robust segmentation even in the presence of noise and artifacts.

5.4.2 Remote Sensing

In remote sensing, random walks help in delineating land cover types and detecting changes in satellite imagery. The method's ability to handle heterogeneous data makes it suitable for complex scenes.

5.4.3 Object Detection

Random walks facilitate object detection in cluttered environments by leveraging spatial relationships and context. This is particularly useful in applications such as autonomous driving and surveillance.

5.4.4 Texture Segmentation

For texture segmentation, random walks excel by modeling the local intensity variations and spatial coherence. This enables the accurate segmentation of regions with distinct textures.

5.5 Advantages and Limitations

5.5.1 Advantages

- Robustness: Random walks are resilient to noise and variations in image intensity.
- Flexibility: The method can be adapted to various types of images and segmentation tasks.
- Probabilistic Framework: Provides a clear probabilistic interpretation of the segmentation results.

5.5.2 Limitations

- Computational Complexity: Solving the system of linear equations can be computationally expensive for large images.
- Seed Selection: The accuracy of the segmentation heavily depends on the choice of seed points.

5.6 Future Directions

Research in random walks for image segmentation continues to evolve. Future directions include:

- Hybrid Methods: Combining random walks with other segmentation techniques to enhance performance.
- Deep Learning Integration: Leveraging deep learning models to improve the weight calculation and seed selection processes.

- Real-Time Applications: Developing efficient algorithms for real-time segmentation in applications such as video processing and augmented reality.

5.7 Conclusion

Random walks offer a powerful and versatile approach to image segmentation, capable of handling noise and complex structures. By leveraging the probabilistic nature of random walks, we can achieve accurate and reliable segmentation results across various domains.

References

1. Grady, L. (2006). Random walks for image segmentation. IEEE Transactions on Pattern Analysis and Machine Intelligence, 28(11), 1768-1783.

2. Li, X., Sun, X., Meng, G., & Ma, L. (2013). Random walk and graph cut for co-segmentation of multiple images. IEEE Transactions on Image Processing, 22(1), 285-299.

3. Mortensen, E. N., & Barrett, W. A. (1998). Interactive segmentation with intelligent scissors. Graphical Models and Image Processing, 60(5), 349-384.

4. Boykov, Y., & Jolly, M. P. (2001). Interactive graph cuts for optimal boundary & region segmentation of objects in N-D images. In Proceedings of the Eighth IEEE International Conference on Computer Vision (Vol. 1, pp. 105-112).

5. Vicente, S., Rother, C., & Kolmogorov, V. (2008). Object cosegmentation. In IEEE Conference on Computer Vision and Pattern Recognition (pp. 1-8).

Epilogue

The exploration of stochastic processes and pattern recognition in image processing presented in this book highlights the power of probabilistic modeling in handling uncertainty, noise, and complexity in visual data analysis. From fundamental mathematical principles to advanced machine learning techniques, this book has bridged the gap between theoretical foundations and practical applications, making it a valuable resource for students, researchers, and professionals working in computer vision, AI, and digital image processing.

The integration of stochastic methods into image processing enables more robust and adaptive algorithms that can enhance feature extraction, classification, and segmentation tasks. By leveraging techniques such as Markov models, Bayesian inference, and probabilistic graphical models, we gain deeper insights into the underlying structure of image data, enabling better decision-making in various applications, including medical imaging, remote sensing, and autonomous systems.

Pattern recognition, a cornerstone of intelligent image analysis, has evolved significantly with the advent of deep learning and probabilistic approaches. The ability to identify and classify patterns using stochastic techniques has paved the way for more efficient image interpretation, object recognition, and automated decision-making. By combining traditional statistical models with modern AI-driven methodologies, this book has outlined how cutting-edge research continues to push the boundaries of what is possible in image processing.

Image segmentation, a crucial step in image analysis, benefits greatly from stochastic frameworks, such as random walks, Markov random fields, and probabilistic clustering. These techniques allow for accurate object separation, edge detection, and region-based analysis, which are essential in applications like medical diagnostics, security, and industrial automation. The use of graph-based probabilistic models further enhances the precision and efficiency of segmentation methods, making them more adaptable to complex and real-world imaging challenges.

As technology advances, the fusion of stochastic processes with deep learning will continue to shape the future of computer vision and artificial intelligence. The ability to train models that understand and adapt to uncertain environments will become increasingly important, opening up new frontiers in autonomous systems, augmented reality, and intelligent surveillance. The insights and methodologies discussed in this book provide a strong foundation for further research and development in these areas, encouraging the exploration of hybrid models that combine probabilistic reasoning with neural network-based approaches.

In conclusion, stochastic processes and pattern recognition are essential tools for advancing the field of image processing, offering both theoretical depth and practical utility. This book has aimed to equip readers with the knowledge, techniques, and motivation to further explore and contribute to this dynamic and rapidly evolving domain. As we move forward, the intersection of probabilistic models, AI, and computational imaging will continue to drive groundbreaking innovations, redefining how machines perceive and interpret the world around us.

www.ingramcontent.com/pod-product-compliance
Lightning Source LLC
LaVergne TN
LVHW041256150826
845673LV00008B/2607

* 9 7 9 8 8 9 7 2 4 6 0 1 4 *